So, You Want to "Do Hair" –What Is NOT Taught
In Cosmetology School©
by Sondra Y. Hill-Ward

Table of Contents

Introduction

Acknowledgements and Dedication

My Story

Chapter 1......................... Choosing a School and Obtaining your License

Chapter 2...............Doing it Right (Taxes and Establishing Your Business)
1. What is a "Form of business"?
2. What Taxes Will I Have to Pay?
3. Your Business Team

Chapter 3.. Supplies and Tools of the Trade

Chapter 4.. Booth Rental vs Owning

Chapter 5.. Building Your Clientele

Final Thoughts

Business Checklist

Resources

About the Author

INTRODUCTION

I was a Cosmetologist (1986-2001) and still am one in my heart. What!!!!!?? Yes, I no longer actively practice this art form; but, once you have learned your craft including mistakes made by you and others in this field or any other business for that matter, you NEVER forget what it takes to do it successfully.

I earned a great salary and when God said, "Time to stop"; I did just that with no regret. What I did not know was that I would end up using my experience to help others in book form.

You will see some of my blog posts inserted where applicable. My blog information is listed at the end of this guide.

It is my prayer that the information on the next few pages brings you even more success as you endeavor to greatness in this field called, Cosmetology. Blessings.

ACKNOWLEDGEMENTS

I can do nothing apart from God. He gave me the vision to start writing this book along with all other abilities that I possess. I want to always hear and do His will in my life.

Thank you is not enough for the support that my husband, Derek Dean Ward, II. He is my friend, cheerleader, and challenger.

Dean, you always calm me when I am overwhelmed and feeling "flighty", which is a lot.

In 2014, I joined a newly-formed elite group of business women who encouraged and directed me in the writing of this book at a divine time and I am enriched by every member. #V40

DEDICATION

I come from a line of Cosmetologists which include my maternal Grandmother, Elizabeth Hayes Clayton, Aunts, and Cousins on both sides of my lineage. I pay homage to them who when you could "do hair" in the kitchen, paved the way for me to become a licensed Cosmetologist.

I saved the best for last for I dedicate this book to my parents, the late Laura Evelyn Clayton Hill and Wilbert Frank Hill. Their love for me is felt for an eternity and beyond. I do not doubt that they are proud of their baby daughter and I miss them more than anyone will ever know. They set the foundation and work ethic that exists within me.

God blessed me with, in my opinion (which is the only one that counts) the best of the best.

My Story

For two years I did not file taxes or have an established business at all. All I did was spend the money that was made. It took about five years into a 16-year Cosmetology career for me to really understand how money worked. When I stopped this career path, I had little to show for it monetarily. I did implement some good financial habits, but it was not enough.

Fast forward to about 2001 and I had a total mind shift. I researched and planned to be self employed again (really missed it). I started to talk to people who were doing well as entrepreneurs and learned so much.

I finally acted in 2013 when the opportunity for me to step out again. I knew now how to file, what to file, and everything that it took to establish business and not be "bootleg" anymore.

As I started to meet and talk to people who were Cosmetologists, I found out that nothing had changed as far as Cosmetologists not knowing or understanding how to organize their business.

So with this in mind, I decided to develop this product and service for student and professional people in the Beauty Industry.

My goal is to educate and change minds about the need to stop cheating yourself while thinking that you are cheating the IRS.

For me, it has been a total turn around in my finances now that I have put the correct and legal practices in place and implement them.

Chapter 1
Choosing a School and Obtaining a License

It's simple: **DO YOUR RESEARCH**!

You Can ask friends and family or go online, research and ask questions about what you need to obtain a great, not good education.

This is your future career. Make sure you receive what your pay for.

To solidify any information you receive, be it word of mouth or the school(s)you interview, your State Board of Cosmetology can help. All legitimate schools are licensed by the state and must comply with rules set forth by that state.

Visit the school(s) that you are interested in and ask questions like:

- What can they do to help you get your license?

- How long does it take to finish?

- How do they make you "state board" ready?

- Do they offer employment assistance?

- Pass/fail rate of their students.

- Find out all fees and when you are supposed to pay them

- Financial assistance, i.e.: federal loans and/or grants.

Compare the answers given to the information you obtain by the state board so that you will know that the business is legitimate in its actions. Should you find discrepancies, you may file a complaint with your state board of cosmetology.

If you have done a through job with this, you should be well on your way to receiving the training that you will need for your career in Cosmetology.

NOTES

Chapter 2

Doing it Right (Taxes and Establishing Your Business)

Yeah, baby!!!!! You got your license! I know it was a lot of work and well worth it!

Congratulations!!!!!! Time to do some more work.

Long before your last months of training, you should have been looking for the salon with which you want to work or deciding if you want to open your own salon. Here are some things to consider:

- Do you have enough knowledge about this field to just jump in and open for business or is more information needed?

- Are you willing to go through the process needed to hire and/or fire someone?

- Who are your customers?

These are only a few things that you need to think about. I can say this, regardless as to what you decide, I can only suggest that you work in a salon first while you decide. I say this because you can learn a lot from established business owners as you hone your skills. It's up to you to do what you are comfortable with.

If you want success......the right way, decide how you are going to conduct business. What I mean is choose a form of business (LLC, corporation, etc.). Like I stated in the previous chapter to make the right choices for you, you will have to do research and find out what each form of business does. This is so important when filing taxes. OK, YOU

MUST FILE TAXES IF YOU ARE IN BUSINESS. Sorry for shouting but; many Cosmetologists, at some point in time (including yours truly) did not do what they should have done where this is concerned. I got my act together and believe me, it was the best business move that I made.

1. What is a "Form of business"?

You should consider what form of business you want to start. I will list them and a brief description of the benefits they will afford you, the business owner.

Limited Liability Company-LLC

A business entity organized in the United States under state law. An LLC may be classified for federal incomes tax as a partnership, corporation, an entity separate form its owner. You do **not** work for the LLC but are subject to taxes on the earnings from self-employment of the LLC, which is treated the same as a sole-proprietorship. If you have employee(s), there are taxes which must be paid such as FICA and Social Security, to name a few.

A LLC separates you, the owner from your company and allows more tax benefits which keep you from paying more or an increase in taxes.

Partnerships

An unincorporated organization with two or more members is generally classified as a partnership for federal tax purposes if its members carry on a trade, business financial operation or venture and **divide** its **profits**. **However**, a joint undertaking merely to share expenses is **not** a partnership.

Corporations

A "C" corporation is a separate entity for income tax purposes. It files a corporation income tax return where it reports it profit or loss and pays income taxes at the corporate income tax rate based on its profits. Distributions of profits in the form of dividends hold the potential for double taxation.

A "S" corporation distributes profits and the income is taxed only at the individual shareholders rate, with no tax liability to the company itself. Any losses can be passed on to the shareholders, who can use them to offset other income they have.

The above definitions are only a "brief" explanation of the different forms of business. It would be wise to have your accountant explain these in detail. You should also look them up on line (irs.gov) or visit your local library.

What Taxes Will I Have to Pay?

Taxes paid for doing business varies from state to state. Check with your local state revenue service and your accountant for any specific information needed.

- Federal Taxes- Taxes on the business itself. Income from proprietorships, partnerships or other unincorporated business is subject to individual income taxes of the owners using form 1040 with appropriate schedules. Incorporated businesses are subject to U. S. corporate income tax laws.

- State Tax- Like federal income tax, the state also requires that income from proprietorships, partnerships, of other unincorporated businesses be taxed at the state individual income tax rate of the owners.

- Sales, Use and Business Tax- E-commerce and mail order sales tax rulings, as well information regarding who collects an enforces taxes in your state.

- Employment Tax- Employment taxes can generally fit into three categories: those taxes you must pay for each employee, taxes you must withhold from each employee's pay and workmen's compensation (not a tax but an expense related to employment).

- Tax Numbers- Federal employer identification Tax number (EIN). Every person who pays wages to one or more employees and who has not previously secured an identification number. Must be filed by those who wish to pay wages on or before the seventh day after the date on which business begins.

- State Sales Tax Number- Anyone who sells tangible personal property to an end user and collect sales tax must have this number as governed by your state.

- Income Tax Withholding Number- Any business that hires employees and pays wages needs a income tax withholding number as governed by your state.

- Unemployment Compensation Tax Number- Needed if an injury is incurred by someone in your company. This number is filed with the Department of Industrial Relations.

Your Business Team

What I Did Not Know About Establishing Business

I was a Cosmetologist for 16 years in the State of Alabama. All I knew at that time was that I wanted to work for myself and no one else, PERIOD that's all!

I found out as I went through that there is more to it than just purchasing supplies, obtaining a license, and standing behind a styling chair. I needed to have established my business so that I could have taken advantage of the tax breaks.

In the Cosmetology Industry it is easy to go through your entire career and NOT PAY TAXES. This is the worst thing that I could have done, and I did just that for 2 years which means that I could not prove legally that I even had a job.

When I learned what I needed to do. Here are three things you can do to avoid having problems:

1. Claim ALL your income. When you under report, it looks like you do not make enough income and lending institutions will not approve a loan.
2. Organize your receipts. It makes for uncomplicated record keeping when it is time to file taxes.
3. Hire a CPA. Certified Public Accountants keep up with changing tax laws and have systems in place to help you keep tax audits from happening.
4. Hire a BUSINESS Attorney for ANY business legal needs.

It's not too late to get your business life organized so that you can concentrate on "Doing Hair"! I wish I knew then what I am advising you now.

Chapter 3
Supplies and Tools of the Trade

Even before I finished my training, I started purchasing supplies needed to get started. You should have what is called a starter kit when you enroll in school so all you will need to do is add to what you have.

A starter kit should include rollers (various sizes), shears, and permanent wave rods (various sizes), and shampoo cape. There are other items included to start your inventory. Make sure that you invest in quality products and implements (tools). Quality tools make a huge difference in how well you do your job.

Understanding ingredients and how they affect hair puts you above the rest and is better than just knowing that "it works". Anybody can say that. You need to know why products and tools do what they do and be able to articulate as much. There is more than enough room for intelligence as well as talent. Attend as many industry trade shows as you can. Take advance haircutting and styling classes. Get all the continuing education available to you.

While you are in school and after graduation, enter competitions locally and in different states. Your knowledge base will increase as well as your reputation. Having as much knowledge as you can will help you represent your trade well. The tools of the trade include continuing education as well as the physical combs, brushes, shears, etcetera; that are used daily. The Cosmetology industry is always evolving and changing, and you will never stop learning, if you want to excel.

NOTES

Chapter 4
Booth Rental versus Owning

You can do one of three things:

- Open your own salon

- Booth rent

- Allow the salon owner to provide supplies and pay you a percentage of the daily/weekly earnings, (ex. 50%-50%, 60%-40%, etc.)

There may be other ways; these are the ones that I know about.

Either way, you will need to keep up with your expenses. Most people choose to booth rent which is a business within a business. You have not only taxes but in some cases equipment may or may not be provided. However, you decide to function in business, read your contract.... yes, there should be a written contract that you both agree upon.

If one is not provided, write one yourself and have everyone involved sign it. If you can't get cooperation, run, don't walk out of the door. You must protect yourself legally.

Do the work needed so that you can do what you love without many or any problems.

Your state board of cosmetology and your accountant are the best resources for information and guidance.

Mind Shift

Cosmetologists/Barbers are businesses in and of themselves. Having insurances to cover their business and personal interests is all too important. Having a mentor or seeking guidance from someone who has had the success that you aspire to is important in your mind shift journey.

Continued education makes you an expert in your field thus drawing clients to you to solve their hair care problems.

Your thoughts about your vocation come thru in the way you think of your business. Think of yourself as a **professional** and not just a trade. You can effect change that everyone can **see** (objective). You also effect change that cannot be seen (subjective). It makes your client **feel** great when his/her hair looks great.

- You are a business within a business when you rent a space in which to work.
- You are a business entity as a Cosmetologist/Barber, you are responsible for state, local, and federal taxes.
- You should set up your business as a legal business entity.
- You should have a clear understanding of front end expenses of being a Cosmetologist/Barber.

Chapter 5
Building Your Clientele

I know that whoever does my hair well and understands everything about what it takes to make my hair HEALTHY as well as the ability to make me look good……. I will follow them to the ends of the earth!!!

You know how you are about your dentist, medical doctor, and anyone else that makes your life better, clients feel the same way about their hair, some more than the doctor or dentist.

There are many ways to draw business. Bring a friend and pay one price or approaching someone who is in the public eye daily and offering to do their free….yes free (it's tax deductible !) so you can advertise your work. You must be as creative in advertising as you are at "doing hair".

Word of mouth is by far the best, but; you must give people something to talk about……something positive I mean. People will ask, "Who did your hair?" for two reasons, either they like it and want to patronize you or they want to tell others to "STAY AWAY!!".

You may even want to target a certain kind of client. When I was in business, I only did teenagers and children **if** they were related or the client and asked if I would "do their grandchild's/ daughter/niece's/friend's hair". So, you can say that my **target** client was the 'professional woman'.

Your clientele………. your choice.

5 Tips BEFORE Taking Your First Client

I know, you just want to DO HAIR. There are things…. business things that need to be done so that you will not HAVE to stand behind a chair for the rest of your life. You do want to retire at some point. Here are 5 things that you should do.

1. **Establish yourself as a business.** - This means that you need to have all your licenses to practice your craft.
2. **Know your startup costs.** - Rollers cost money. How much are you going to spend on them and other supplies that you will need?
3. **Research the insurances and benefits you need to stay in business.** - Even if you don't or can't purchase them immediately, most can't (I couldn't), make plans in the very near future to do so. You'll thank me later.
4. **Know your ideal customer.** - Who do you want to serve? Yes, starting out you may have to service anyone who will pay you. Give yourself time to choose from the clients that you will service, then choose. You may only want to cater to professional clients, men, or children.
5. **Know your brand and setting for your salon or booth.** – Who do you want to represent? How do you want to present yourself so that you can attract the client(s) that you want to serve? If you dress professionally, you will more than likely attract that kind of client. Salon atmosphere is important also.

There are so many things to consider BEFORE announcing that you are in business. Planning is everything. If you don't know what to do, ask someone who is SUCCESSFUL at what you want to do.

Final Thoughts

I want nothing but success for your endeavors in the Cosmetology profession. Be wise in your decisions concerning this business and ask questions. There are never enough great Cosmetologists and there is no reason for you not to be on top in your career.

Make your plan and follow thru.

Business Checklist

Background work

  assess your strengths and weakness
  establish business and personal goals
  identify the financial risks
  assess financial resources
  determine start-up costs
  decide on your business location
  do market research
  identify your customers
  identify your competitors
  develop a marketing plan

Business transactions

  select a lawyer
  choose a form of organization (proprietorship, partnership, for example)
  create your business (register your name, incorporate the business, etc.)
  select an accountant
  prepare a business plan
  select a banker (business account, investments, Roth IRA)
  set up a business checking account
  apply for business loans☐
  establish a line of credit
  select an insurance agent (life, short and long-term disability)
  obtain business insurance (key turners)

First step
   business cards
   review local business codes
   obtain a lease
   line up suppliers☐
   get equipment
   obtain business license or permit☐
   get a federal employer identification number☐
   get a state employer identification number☐
   federal an state tax forms
   join a professional organization
   set a starting date
 ☐ **if applicable**

Resources

Need:	Go to:
Obtaining and Registering Business Name State Tax Formation of Business	Your state department of revenue
Registration of Business	Local probate court/City Hall
Selecting Cosmetology School	Your state board of cosmetology
Employee Identification Number (EIN)	irs.gov

All states have different rules and regulations which govern starting businesses as well as schools of cosmetology. All are available online and by phone. Utilize your local government website for any questions as well as asking established business owner(s). Fees vary from state to state. The information in this document is intended as a guide only and does not in any way guarantee success in the Cosmetology field.

NOTES

ABOUT THE AUTHOR

Sondra Yvonne Hill-Ward, a former Master Cosmetologists and Salon Manager was born and raised in Birmingham, AL and has held many diverse occupations, which include railroad conductor, Best Selling Author, and automotive quality inspector/ assembly line plant employee, and phlebotomist. She resides in Bessemer, AL with her husband.

Contact info:

Website:	proconsult26.com
Email:	proconsult26@nandiventures.com
Facebook Group:	facebook.com/groups/soyouwanttodohair
Twitter:	twitter.com/@sondrayhillward
Blog:	**sondrayhill-ward.blogspot.com**

NOTES

www.ingramcontent.com/pod-product-compliance
Lightning Source LLC
Chambersburg PA
CBHW032311240526
45464CB00023BA/2987